contents

Corn & Red Pepper Chowder

MAKES: 6 SERVINGS ■ **PREP:** 5 MINUTES ■ **COOK:** 45 MINUTES

- 2 tablespoons vegetable oil
- 1 large sweet onion, diced (about 2 cups)
- ¼ cup all-purpose flour
- 2 cloves garlic, minced
- 6 cups Swanson® Chicken Broth (Regular, Natural Goodness® **or** Certified Organic)
- 2 medium Yukon Gold potatoes, diced (about 2 cups)
- 2 cups fresh corn kernels **or** 1 package (10 ounces) frozen whole kernel corn
- 1 jar (7 ounces) roasted red peppers, drained and chopped
- ½ cup heavy cream (optional)
- ⅓ cup chopped fresh basil leaves

1. Heat the oil in a 4-quart saucepan over medium heat. Add the onion and cook until tender. Stir in the flour and garlic. Cook and stir for 1 minute.

2. Stir in the broth and potatoes. Heat to a boil. Reduce the heat to low. Cook for 20 minutes or until the potatoes are tender.

3. Stir the corn and red peppers into the saucepan. Cook for 10 minutes more.

4. Add the cream, if desired, and ¼ **cup** of the basil. Season to taste. Divide the soup among **6** serving bowls. Sprinkle **each** serving of soup with the remaining basil.

French Onion Soup

MAKES: 4 SERVINGS ■ **PREP:** 10 MINUTES ■ **COOK:** 45 MINUTES

1 tablespoon vegetable oil	4 cups Swanson® Beef Broth
¾ pound onions, cut in half and thinly sliced (about 2½ cups)	(Regular, 50% Less Sodium or Certified Organic)
¼ teaspoon sugar	¼ cup dry white wine **or** dry vermouth
2 tablespoons all-purpose flour	4 slices French bread, toasted
	½ cup shredded Swiss cheese

1. Heat the oil in a 6-quart saucepot over low heat. Add the onions. Cover and cook for 15 minutes. **Uncover**.

2. Add the sugar to the saucepot and increase the heat to medium. Cook for 15 minutes or until the onions are golden.

3. Stir in the flour. Cook and stir for 1 minute. Add broth and wine. Heat to a boil. Reduce the heat to low. Cook for 10 minutes.

4. Divide the soup among **4** serving bowls. Top **each** serving of soup with bread and cheese.

TIME-SAVING TIP

Use a food processor with slicing attachment for slicing the onions.

KITCHEN TIP

For added flavor, rub the bread with a peeled garlic clove before toasting.

Hearty Chicken Tortilla Soup

MAKES: 6 SERVINGS ■ **PREP:** 10 MINUTES ■ **COOK:** 30 MINUTES

Vegetable cooking spray

1 pound skinless, boneless chicken breasts, cut into 1-inch pieces

3½ cups Swanson® Chicken Broth (Regular, Natural Goodness® or Certified Organic)

1 teaspoon ground cumin

½ cup **uncooked** regular long-grain white rice

1 can (11 ounces) whole kernel corn with red and green peppers, drained

1 cup Pace® Chunky Salsa

1 tablespoon chopped fresh cilantro leaves

2 tablespoons fresh lime juice
Crisp Tortilla Strips

1. Spray a 6-quart saucepot with cooking spray. Heat over medium-high heat for 1 minute. Add the chicken to the saucepot. Cook until it's browned, stirring often.

2. Stir in the broth, cumin and rice. Heat to a boil. Reduce the heat to low. Cover and cook for 20 minutes.

3. Stir in the corn, salsa, cilantro and lime juice. Cook until the rice is tender. Top **each** serving of soup with Crisp Tortilla Strips.

CRISP TORTILLA STRIPS: Heat the oven to 425°F. Cut **4** corn tortillas into thin strips and place them on a baking sheet. Spray with cooking spray. Bake for 10 minutes or until golden.

KITCHEN TIP

Use a pastry wheel when cutting the tortillas to create a special touch for the soup garnish.

Crab and Corn Chowder

MAKES: 6 SERVINGS ⬛ **PREP:** 5 MINUTES ⬛ **COOK:** 35 MINUTES

- 4 slices bacon
- 1 large sweet onion, coarsely chopped (about 2 cups)
- 2 cloves garlic, minced
- 6 cups Swanson® Chicken Broth (Regular, Natural Goodness® **or** Certified Organic)
- 2 teaspoons seafood seasoning
- 6 to 8 red-skinned regular **or** fingerling potatoes, cut into 1-inch pieces (about 2 cups)
- 2 cups frozen whole kernel corn
- 1 container (8 ounces) refrigerated pasteurized lump crabmeat
- ½ cup heavy cream

1. Cook the bacon in a 4-quart saucepan over medium-high heat for 5 minutes or until the bacon is crisp. Remove the bacon with a fork or kitchen tongs and drain on paper towels. Crumble and set aside. Pour off all but **2 tablespoons** drippings.

2. Reduce the heat to medium. Add the onion and garlic and cook in the hot bacon drippings until tender.

3. Stir in the broth, seafood seasoning, potatoes and corn. Heat to a boil. Reduce the heat to low. Cook for 15 minutes or until the potatoes are tender.

4. Add the crabmeat and cream. Cook for 5 minutes. Divide the chowder among **6** serving bowls. Top **each** with about **1 tablespoon** of the bacon.

Potato Soup with Arugula

MAKES: 6 SERVINGS ■ **PREP:** 15 MINUTES ■ **COOK:** 35 MINUTES

2 tablespoons olive oil

2 leeks, white parts only, cleaned and chopped

4 medium potatoes, peeled and diced

3 cups Swanson® Chicken Broth (Regular, Natural Goodness® or Certified Organic)

1 cup baby arugula

¼ cup heavy cream

2 teaspoons lemon juice

1. Heat the oil in a 4-quart saucepan over medium heat. Add the leeks and cook for 5 minutes. Add the potatoes and cook for 10 minutes or until the potatoes are almost tender.

2. Add the broth. Heat to a boil. Reduce the heat to low. Cover and cook for 20 minutes or until the potatoes are tender. Add the arugula. Cook for 1 minute.

3. Place ½ of the broth mixture into an electric blender or food processor container. Cover and blend until smooth. Pour the mixture into a medium bowl. Repeat the blending process with the remaining broth mixture. Return all of the puréed mixture to the saucepan. Cook over medium heat until the mixture is hot. Season to taste. Stir in the cream and lemon juice. Serve immediately.

KITCHEN TIP

This savory soup is also delicious served cold. Refrigerate for at least 3 hours or until well chilled.

Twice-Baked Potato Soup

MAKES: 8 SERVINGS   ■   **PREP:** 10 MINUTES   ■   **COOK:** 45 MINUTES

6 large baking potatoes, scrubbed and pricked with a fork

2 tablespoons butter

1 small sweet onion, finely chopped (about ½ cup)

5 cups Swanson® Chicken Broth (Regular, Natural Goodness® **or** Certified Organic)

¼ cup light cream

1 tablespoon chopped fresh chives

Potato Toppers

1. Heat the oven to 425°F. Arrange the potatoes on a rack and bake for 30 minutes or until tender. Place the potatoes in a bowl with a lid and let steam. Remove the skin and mash pulp.

2. Heat the butter in a 3-quart saucepan. Add the onion and cook until tender. Add the broth and **5 cups** of the potato pulp.

3. Place ⅓ of the broth mixture into an electric blender or food processor container. Cover and blend until smooth. Place in a medium bowl. Repeat the blending process with the remaining broth mixture. Return all of the puréed mixture into the saucepan. Stir in the cream and chives and cook for 5 minutes more. Season to taste.

4. Place ¼ **cup** of the remaining pulp mixture in each of **8** serving bowls. Divide the broth mixture among the bowls. Serve with one or more *Potato Toppers.*

POTATO TOPPERS: Cooked crumbled bacon, shredded Cheddar cheese **and/or** sour cream.

TIME-SAVING TIP

Microwave the potatoes on HIGH for 10 to 12 minutes or until fork-tender.

Black Bean, Corn & Turkey Chili

MAKES: 6 SERVINGS ■ **PREP:** 15 MINUTES ■ **COOK:** 40 MINUTES

1 tablespoon vegetable oil
1 pound ground turkey
1 medium onion, chopped (about 1 cup)
2 tablespoons chili powder
1 teaspoon ground cumin
½ teaspoon ground black pepper

1¾ cups Swanson® Chicken Broth (Regular, Natural Goodness® **or** Certified Organic)
1 cup Pace® Chunky Salsa
1 can (16 ounces) whole kernel corn, drained
1 can (about 15 ounces) black beans, rinsed and drained

1. Heat the oil in a 4-quart saucepan over medium-high heat. Add the turkey, onion, chili powder, cumin and black pepper. Cook until the turkey is well browned, stirring frequently to separate the meat.

2. Stir in the broth, salsa, corn and beans. Heat to a boil. Reduce the heat to low. Cover and cook for 30 minutes.

Roasted Chicken & Noodle Soup

MAKES: 6 SERVINGS ■ **PREP:** 10 MINUTES ■ **COOK:** 20 MINUTES

1 rotisserie cooked chicken (about 1½ pounds)

2 teaspoons vegetable oil

2 medium onions, halved and thinly sliced (about 1 cup)

8 cups Swanson® Chicken Broth (Regular, Natural Goodness® or Certified Organic)

⅛ teaspoon ground black pepper

2 medium carrots, sliced (about 1 cup)

2 stalks celery, sliced (about 1 cup)

¾ cup **uncooked** trumpet-shaped pasta (campanelle)

1. Remove the skin and bones from the chicken. Cut up enough of the chicken into strips to yield about 2 cups.

2. Heat the oil in a 10-inch skillet over medium-high heat. Add the onions and stir to coat with oil. When the onions begin to brown, reduce the heat to medium. Cook until onions are tender and caramelized, stirring occasionally. Remove from the heat.

3. Meanwhile, heat the broth, black pepper, carrots and celery in a 4-quart saucepan over medium-high heat to a boil.

4. Stir in the pasta and chicken. Reduce the heat to medium. Cook for 10 minutes or until the pasta is tender but still firm. Stir in the onions and serve immediately.

Vegetable Minestrone Soup

MAKES: 8 SERVINGS ■ **PREP:** 10 MINUTES ■ **COOK:** 30 MINUTES

- 2 tablespoons olive **or** vegetable oil
- 2 medium zucchini, cut in half lengthwise and thickly sliced (about 3 cups)
- 2 cloves garlic, minced
- ½ teaspoon dried rosemary leaves, crushed
- 4 cups Swanson® Vegetable Broth (Regular **or** Certified Organic)
- 1 can (about 14.5 ounces) diced tomatoes, drained
- 1 can (about 19 ounces) white kidney (cannellini) beans, rinsed and drained
- ½ cup **uncooked** corkscrew-shaped pasta (rotini)
- ¼ cup grated Parmesan cheese (optional)

1. Heat the oil in a 6-quart saucepot. Add the zucchini, garlic and rosemary and cook until tender-crisp.

2. Add the broth and tomatoes. Heat to a boil. Reduce the heat to low. Cover and cook for 10 minutes.

3. Stir in the beans and pasta. Cook for 10 minutes or until the pasta is tender but still firm. Serve with cheese, if desired.

Sweet Potato & Pecan Soup

MAKES: 8 SERVINGS ■ **PREP:** 30 MINUTES ■ **COOK:** 30 MINUTES

- 2 tablespoons unsalted butter
- 1 large sweet onion, chopped (about 2 cups)
- 4 cloves garlic, minced
- 6 cups Swanson® Vegetable Broth (Regular **or** Certified Organic)
- 2 bay leaves

- 3 large sweet potatoes, peeled and cut into cubes (about 6 cups)
- ¼ teaspoon ground black pepper
- 1 cup heavy cream, divided
- 3 tablespoons thinly sliced fresh chives
- 1 cup pecans, toasted

1. Heat the butter in a 6-quart saucepot over medium heat. Add the onion and garlic and cook until the onion is tender. Add the broth, bay leaves, potatoes and black pepper. Heat to a boil. Reduce the heat to low. Cover and cook for 20 minutes or until the potatoes are tender. Discard the bay leaves. Add ½ **cup** of the cream and heat through.

2. Place ⅓ of the broth mixture in an electric blender or food processor container. Cover and blend until smooth. Pour the mixture into a large bowl. Repeat the blending process twice more with the remaining broth mixture. Return all of the puréed mixture to the saucepot. Cook over medium heat for 5 minutes or until hot. Season to taste.

3. Prepare the *Chive Chantilly*. Beat the remaining heavy cream in a medium bowl with an electric mixer on high speed until stiff peaks form. Gently stir in the chives. Serve with the soup and sprinkle with the pecans.

Cream of Roasted Fennel Soup

MAKES: 8 SERVINGS ■ **PREP:** 10 MINUTES ■ **BAKE:** 30 MINUTES ■ **COOK:** 10 MINUTES

- 3 **bulbs fennel, cut into ½-inch slices**
- 2 **large onions, cut into ½-inch slices**
- 2 **cloves garlic, minced**
- ¼ **teaspoon cracked black pepper**
- 2 **tablespoons olive oil**
- 5¼ **cups Swanson® Vegetable Broth (Regular or Certified Organic)**
- ½ **cup heavy cream**
- ¼ **cup coarsely chopped fresh basil leaves**

1. Heat the oven to 425°F. Place the fennel, onions, garlic and black pepper in a 17×11-inch roasting pan. Pour the oil over the vegetables and toss to coat. Bake for 30 minutes or until the vegetables are tender.

2. Place ½ of the vegetables in a food processor container with **1 cup** of the broth. Cover and blend until smooth. Pour the vegetable mixture into a 4-quart saucepan. Repeat the blending process with the remaining vegetables and **1 cup** of the broth.

3. Stir the remaining broth, cream and basil into the saucepan. Cook over low heat for 10 minutes, stirring occasionally. Season to taste with additional black pepper.

KITCHEN TIP

Trim the base of each fennel bulb. Remove the stalks and greenery for other uses, such as salads. Wash and slice fennel bulbs for soup.

Grilled Asparagus Soup

MAKES: 6 SERVINGS ■ **PREP:** 10 MINUTES ■ **GRILL:** 8 MINUTES ■ **COOK:** 25 MINUTES

1½ **pounds asparagus spears, trimmed**

3 **tablespoons olive oil**

¼ **teaspoon cracked black pepper**

1 **large sweet onion, chopped (about 2 cups)**

2 **cloves garlic, minced**

2 **tablespoons all-purpose flour**

6 **cups Swanson® Vegetable Broth (Regular or Certified Organic)**

1 **tablespoon chopped fresh rosemary leaves**

Fresh rosemary sprigs (optional)

1. Place the asparagus in a single layer on a large platter. Drizzle with **1 tablespoon** of the oil and black pepper. Toss to coat. Heat the grill to medium. Place a perforated grill pan on the grill rack. Place the asparagus on the pan in a single layer and grill for 8 minutes or until the asparagus is tender-crisp, turning halfway through cooking. Remove from heat. Cool.

2. Heat the remaining oil in a 4-quart saucepan over medium heat. Add the onion and garlic and cook until tender-crisp. Meanwhile, cut the asparagus diagonally into 1-inch pieces. Set aside. Reduce the heat to low. Add the flour to the onion mixture. Cook for 5 minutes, stirring often. Gradually stir in the broth. Heat to a boil. Reduce the heat to low. Cover and cook for 10 minutes or until the onion is tender. Stir in **half** of the cut asparagus pieces.

3. Purée broth mixture in three batches until smooth. Return mixture to the saucepan. Add the remaining asparagus and rosemary. Cook over medium heat until the mixture is hot. Garnish with rosemary sprig, if desired.

CREAMY GRILLED ASPARAGUS SOUP

*Add ½ **cup** half-and-half or heavy cream when reheating soup.*

Zucchini Soup with Herbed Cream

MAKES: 6 SERVINGS ■ **PREP:** 15 MINUTES ■ **COOK:** 30 MINUTES

½ cup sour cream

4 teaspoons chopped fresh basil leaves

4 teaspoons chopped fresh oregano leaves

2 tablespoons olive oil

1 large onion, finely chopped (about 1 cup)

1 clove garlic, minced

4 medium zucchini, thinly sliced (about 10 cups)

¼ teaspoon ground black pepper

3 cups Swanson® Vegetable Broth (Regular **or** Certified Organic)

1. Stir the sour cream, **1 teaspoon** of the basil and **1 teaspoon** of the oregano in a small bowl. Cover and refrigerate.

2. Heat oil in a 4-quart saucepan over medium heat. Add the onion and garlic. Cook until tender. Add the zucchini and black pepper. Cook for about 5 minutes or until tender.

3. Add the broth, remaining basil and oregano. Heat to a boil. Reduce the heat to low. Cover and cook for 15 minutes.

4. Place ⅓ of the zucchini mixture into an electric blender or food processor container. Cover and blend until smooth. Pour the mixture into a large bowl. Repeat the blending process twice more with the remaining zucchini mixture. Return all of the puréed mixture to the saucepan. Cook over medium heat for 5 minutes or until hot.

5. Divide the soup among **6** serving bowls. Add **about 1 tablespoon** of the sour cream mixture into each, using a spoon to swirl the cream on the soup surface.

Madeira Mushroom and Leek Soup

MAKES: 6 SERVINGS ■ **PREP:** 10 MINUTES ■ **STAND:** 30 MINUTES ■ **COOK:** 45 MINUTES

- 6 cups Swanson® Vegetable Broth (Regular **or** Certified Organic)
- ½ cup Madeira wine
- 1 ounce dried shiitake, morel **or** cèpes mushrooms
- 4 tablespoons butter
- 3 leeks, white parts only, cleaned and coarsely chopped (about 2 cups)
- 2 tablespoons all-purpose flour
- 1 package (8 ounces) sliced white mushrooms (about 3 cups)
- ¼ teaspoon ground black pepper
  Sliced mushrooms **and** leeks

1. Heat **1 cup** of the broth, wine and mushrooms in a 1-quart saucepan over high heat to a boil. Remove from the heat. Let stand for 30 minutes. Do not drain.

2. Heat the butter in a 4-quart saucepan over low heat. Add the leeks and cook until tender-crisp. Add the flour. Cook for 5 minutes, stirring often.

3. Gradually stir in the remaining broth, sliced white mushrooms, black pepper and the rehydrated wild mushrooms and liquid. Heat to a boil. Reduce heat to low. Cook for 30 minutes or until the mushrooms are tender.

4. Purée the mushroom mixture in batches until smooth. Return all of the puréed mixture to the saucepan. Cook over medium heat for 5 minutes or until hot.

5. Divide the soup among **6** serving bowls. Garnish with the mushrooms and leeks.

Oven-Roasted Beet Soup with Orange Cream

MAKES: 6 SERVINGS ■ **PREP:** 20 MINUTES ■ **COOK:** 35 MINUTES

½ cup sour cream
1 teaspoon grated orange peel
1 tablespoon packed brown sugar
1 tablespoon orange juice
1 bunch beets (4 to 6), peeled and diced (about 4 cups)
1 pound parsnips, diced

1 medium sweet onion, chopped (about 1 cup)
2 cloves garlic, sliced
2 tablespoons olive oil
5 cups Swanson® Vegetable Broth (Regular **or** Certified Organic)
Orange peel (optional)

1. Stir the sour cream, ½ **teaspoon** of the orange peel, brown sugar and orange juice in a small bowl. Cover and refrigerate.

2. Heat the oven to 425°F. Spread the beets, parsnips, onion and garlic in a single layer in a 17×11-inch roasting pan. Pour the oil over the vegetables and toss to coat. Season to taste. Bake for 25 minutes or until the beets are tender.

3. Place **half** of the vegetable mixture and ½ **cup** of the broth and remaining orange peel into an electric blender or food processor container. Cover and blend until smooth. Pour the puréed mixture into a 3-quart saucepan. Repeat the blending process with the remaining vegetables and ½ **cup** broth. Add to the saucepan with the remaining broth. Cook over high heat to a boil. Reduce the heat to low. Cook for 10 minutes.

4. Divide the soup among **6** serving bowls and top **each** with **about 1 tablespoon** of the sour cream mixture. Serve **each** with orange peel, if desired.

Roasted Tomato & Eggplant Bisque

MAKES: 6 SERVINGS ■ **PREP:** 15 MINUTES ■ **COOK:** 35 MINUTES

- 1 medium eggplant, peeled and diced (about 4 cups)
- 4 large plum tomatoes, cut into quarters
- 2 cloves garlic, sliced
- 1 tablespoon olive oil
- 4 cups Swanson® Vegetable Broth (Regular **or** Certified Organic)
- ½ cup crumbled feta cheese
- 2 tablespoons light cream
- 1 tablespoon thinly sliced fresh basil leaves

1. Heat the oven to 425°F. Arrange the eggplant, tomatoes and garlic in a 13×9-inch roasting pan. Pour the oil over the vegetables and toss to coat. Bake for 25 minutes.

2. Place the vegetable mixture in an electric blender or food processor container with **1 cup** of the broth and ¼ **cup** of the cheese. Cover and blend until smooth. Pour the puréed mixture into a 3-quart saucepan and add the remaining broth. Heat to a boil. Reduce the heat to low. Stir in the cream and basil. Cook for 5 minutes.

3. Divide the soup among **6** serving bowls. Garnish **each** serving of soup with about **2 teaspoons** of the remaining cheese.

Roasted Vegetable Soup with Garlic Herb Drizzle

MAKES: 8 SERVINGS ■ **PREP:** 15 MINUTES ■ **BAKE:** 25 MINUTES ■ **COOK:** 30 MINUTES

1 small bulb garlic
7 tablespoons olive oil
1 pound white potatoes, cut into cubes
1 small bulb fennel, cut into cubes
2 carrots, chopped (about 1 cup)

1 medium sweet onion, chopped (about 1 cup)
6 cups Swanson® Vegetable Broth (Regular **or** Certified Organic)
¼ cup finely chopped fresh basil **and/or** parsley leaves

1. Heat the oven to 425°F. Cut ⅓ off the top of the garlic bulb and discard. Place remaining garlic on a piece of aluminum foil. Drizzle with **1 tablespoon** of the olive oil and wrap. Arrange the potatoes, fennel, carrots and onion in a 17×11-inch roasting pan. Pour **2 tablespoons** of the oil over the vegetables and toss to coat. Season to taste. Bake the vegetables and garlic for 25 minutes.

2. Place **1 cup** of the broth with the vegetable mixture into an electric blender or food processor container. Cover and blend until coarsely puréed. Pour the mixture into a 3-quart saucepan. Add the remaining broth. Cook over high heat to a boil. Reduce the heat to low. Cook for 5 minutes.

3. Peel and smash the garlic in a small bowl. Add the basil and remaining oil.

4. Divide the soup mixture among **8** serving bowls. Top **each** with about **1 tablespoon** of the herbed oil mixture.

Blue Cheese Potato Soup with Olive Tapenade

MAKES: 12 SERVINGS ■ **PREP:** 15 MINUTES ■ **COOK:** 40 MINUTES

- 2 tablespoons olive oil
- 1 medium onion, chopped (about 1 cup)
- 5 cloves garlic, minced
- 6 cups Swanson® Vegetable Broth (Regular **or** Certified Organic)
- 4 pounds red-skinned potatoes, peeled and diced (about 12 cups)
- 1 tablespoon balsamic vinegar
- ⅓ cup crumbled blue cheese
- ½ cup prepared olive tapenade

1. Heat the oil in a 6-quart saucepot over medium heat. Add the onion and garlic and cook until tender.

2. Add the broth and potatoes. Heat to a boil. Reduce the heat to low. Cover and cook for 30 minutes or until the potatoes are tender.

3. Place ⅓ of the broth mixture into an electric blender or food processor container. Cover and blend until smooth. Pour the mixture into a large bowl. Repeat the blending process twice more with the remaining broth mixture. Return all of the puréed mixture to the saucepot. Add the vinegar and the cheese. Cook over medium heat for 5 minutes or until the mixture is hot. Season to taste.

4. Divide the soup mixture among **12** serving bowls and top **each** with **2 teaspoons** of the tapenade.

KITCHEN TIP

Tapenade is a rich condiment made of capers, anchovies, ripe olives, olive oil, lemon juice and seasonings. It can be purchased from the specialty section in most grocery stores.

Mediterranean Fish Soup

MAKES: 6 SERVINGS ■ PREP: 10 MINUTES ■ COOK: 20 MINUTES

2 tablespoons olive oil

1 large sweet onion, chopped (about 2 cups)

¼ cup dry white wine **or** Swanson® Chicken Broth (Regular, Natural Goodness® **or** Certified Organic)

4 cups Swanson® Vegetable **or** Chicken Broth (Regular **or** Certified Organic)

1 can (14.5 ounces) diced tomatoes, undrained

2 dozen mussels, well scrubbed with beards removed

1 pound white fish fillets, cut into 1-inch pieces (halibut, cod **or** scrod)

½ pound large shrimp, shelled and deveined

Shredded fresh basil leaves

1. Heat the oil in a 6-quart saucepot over medium heat. Add the onion and cook until tender.

2. Add the wine and cook for 1 minute. Stir in the broth and tomatoes. Heat to a boil. Reduce the heat to low. Add the mussels, fish and shrimp. Cover and cook until the mussels open, fish flakes easily when tested with a fork and shrimp turn pink. Discard any mussels that do not open. Season to taste. Garnish with the basil.

KITCHEN TIP

Select mussels with tightly closed shells or shells that snap shut when lightly tapped. Avoid those with broken shells. To prepare, scrub mussels with a brush under running water and trim "beards" with kitchen scissors.

Escarole Soup with Chickpeas

MAKES: 6 SERVINGS ■ **PREP:** 15 MINUTES ■ **COOK:** 30 MINUTES

1   slice bacon, chopped

2   cloves garlic, minced

8   cups Swanson® Chicken Broth (Regular, Natural Goodness® or Certified Organic)

1   teaspoon Italian seasoning, crushed

½   cup **uncooked** rice-shaped pasta (orzo)

1   bunch escarole, sliced (about 6 cups)

3   medium fresh tomatoes, chopped (about 1½ cups)

1   can (about 16 ounces) chickpeas (garbanzo beans), rinsed and drained

    Ground black pepper

    Shredded Parmesan cheese

1. Cook the bacon in a 6-quart saucepot over medium heat for 1 minute. Add the garlic and cook until bacon is browned.

2. Add the broth and seasoning. Heat to a boil. Add the pasta. Cover and cook for 10 minutes. Add the escarole, tomatoes and beans. Cook for 10 minutes more or until the escarole is tender. Season with black pepper to taste. Serve with cheese.

Roasted Squash Soup with Crispy Bacon

MAKES: 6 SERVINGS ■ **PREP:** 15 MINUTES ■ **BAKE:** 25 MINUTES ■ **COOK:** 5 MINUTES

- 1 small butternut squash (about 1½ pounds), diced (about 4 cups)
- 2 large onions, sliced (about 2 cups)
- 3 tablespoons olive oil
- 3 cups Swanson® Chicken Broth (Regular, Natural Goodness® or Certified Organic)
- ½ cup heavy cream
- ¼ cup real bacon bits

1. Heat the oven to 425°F. Place the squash and onions in a 17×11-inch roasting pan. Add the oil and toss to coat. Bake for 25 minutes or until the squash is tender.

2. Place ½ of the squash mixture, **1½ cups** of the broth and **¼ cup** of the cream in an electric blender or food processor container. Cover and blend until smooth. Pour the mixture into a medium bowl. Repeat the blending process with the remaining squash mixture, broth and cream. Season to taste. Return all of the puréed mixture to a 3-quart saucepan. Cook over medium heat for 5 minutes or until hot.

3. Divide the soup among **6** serving bowls. Top **each** serving of soup with **2 teaspoons** of the bacon.

EASY SUBSTITUTION TIP

*Substitute **4** slices bacon, cooked and crumbled for the bacon bits.*

TIME-SAVING TIP

Ready-cut butternut squash is sold in 20-ounce bags in the produce section, or you may also find it in the frozen foods section of your supermarket.

Easy Mushroom Soup

MAKES: 4 SERVINGS ■ **PREP:** 15 MINUTES ■ **COOK:** 25 MINUTES

1¾ cups Swanson® Beef Broth (Regular, 50% Less Sodium or Certified Organic)

1¾ cups Swanson® Chicken Broth (Regular, Natural Goodness® or Certified Organic)

⅛ teaspoon ground black pepper

⅛ teaspoon dried rosemary leaves, crushed

8 ounces fresh mushrooms, sliced (about 2 cups)

¼ cup thinly sliced carrots

¼ cup finely chopped onion

¼ cup sliced celery

¼ cup fresh **or** frozen peas

1 tablespoon sliced green onion

1. Heat the broth, black pepper, rosemary, mushrooms, carrots, onion, celery and peas in a 4-quart saucepan over medium heat to a boil. Reduce the heat to low. Cover and cook for 15 minutes.

2. Add the green onion. Cook for 5 minutes more or until the vegetables are tender.

Hearty Lasagna Soup

MAKES: 4 SERVINGS ■ **PREP:** 5 MINUTES ■ **COOK:** 25 MINUTES

- 1 **pound ground beef**
- ¼ **teaspoon garlic powder**
- 3½ **cups Swanson® Seasoned Beef Broth with Onion**
- 1 **can (14.5 ounces) diced tomatoes, undrained**
- ¼ **teaspoon dried Italian seasoning, crushed**
- 1½ **cups uncooked mini lasagna noodle-shaped pasta (mafalda) or corkscrew-shaped pasta (rotini)**
- ¼ **cup grated Parmesan cheese**

1. Cook the beef with garlic powder in a 10-inch skillet over medium-high heat until it's well browned, stirring frequently to separate the meat. Pour off any fat.

2. Stir the broth, tomatoes and Italian seasoning into the skillet. Heat to a boil.

3. Stir in the pasta. Reduce the heat to medium. Cook and stir for 10 minutes or until the pasta is tender but still firm. Stir in the cheese. Serve with additional cheese, if desired.

Roasted Garlic Potato Soup

MAKES: 4 SERVINGS ■ **PREP:** 10 MINUTES ■ **COOK:** 25 MINUTES

3½ cups Swanson® Seasoned
     Chicken Broth with Roasted
     Garlic

  4 medium red potatoes, cut
     into cubes (about 4 cups)

  2 medium carrots, diced
     (about 1 cup)

  1 medium onion, chopped
     (about ½ cup)

  1 stalk celery, chopped
     (about ½ cup)

  2 slices bacon, cooked and
     crumbled

  1 cup milk

  1 cup instant mashed potato
     flakes **or** buds

  1 tablespoon chopped fresh
     parsley

1. Heat the broth, potatoes, carrots, onion, celery and bacon in a 4-quart saucepan. Heat to a boil. Reduce the heat to low. Cover and cook for 15 minutes or until the vegetables are tender. Remove from the heat.

2. Stir in the milk, potato flakes and parsley. Cook over medium heat until the mixture is hot.

Creamy Irish Potato Soup

MAKES: 5 SERVINGS ■ **PREP:** 10 MINUTES ■ **COOK:** 25 MINUTES

- 2 tablespoons butter
- 4 medium green onions, sliced (about ½ cup)
- 1 stalk celery, sliced (about ½ cup)
- 1¾ cups Swanson® Chicken Broth (Regular, Natural Goodness® or Certified Organic)

- ½ cup water
- ⅛ teaspoon ground black pepper
- 3 medium potatoes, sliced ¼-inch thick (about 3 cups)
- 1½ cups milk
- Sliced chives **or** green onions (optional)

1. Heat the butter in a 2-quart saucepan over medium-high heat. Add the green onions and celery and cook until tender.

2. Stir the broth, water, black pepper and potatoes into the saucepan. Heat to a boil. Reduce the heat to low. Cover and cook for 15 minutes more or until the potatoes are tender. Remove from the heat.

3. Place ½ of the broth mixture and ¾ **cup** of the milk into an electric blender container. Cover and blend until smooth. Pour into a medium bowl. Repeat the blending process with the remaining broth mixture and remaining milk. Return all of the puréed mixture to the saucepan. Cook over medium heat until the mixture is hot. Sprinkle with chives, if desired.

Warm Avocado Soup with Chipotle Cream

MAKES: 8 SERVINGS ■ **PREP:** 15 MINUTES ■ **COOK:** 10 MINUTES

1 cup sour cream

¼ teaspoon ground chipotle chile pepper

2 tablespoons olive oil

1 large onion, chopped (about 1 cup)

1 clove garlic, minced

6 cups Swanson® Chicken Broth (Regular, Natural Goodness® **or** Certified Organic)

2 tablespoons chopped fresh cilantro

2 tablespoons lime juice

4 avocados, pitted, peeled and cut into cubes (about 5 cups)

1. Stir the sour cream and chile pepper in a small bowl.

2. Heat the oil in a 6-quart saucepot over medium heat. Add onion and cook for 4 minutes. Add garlic and cook for 30 seconds. Stir the broth, cilantro, lime juice and avocados into the saucepot. Heat to a boil.

3. Place ½ of the avocado mixture in an electric blender or food processor container. Cover and blend until smooth. Pour the mixture into a medium bowl. Repeat the blending process with the remaining avocado mixture. Return all of the puréed mixture to the saucepot. Cook over medium heat until the mixture is hot. Divide the soup among **8** serving bowls. Top **each** with about **1 tablespoon** of the sour cream mixture.

Pork Pozole

MAKES: 6 SERVINGS ■ **PREP:** 15 MINUTES ■ **COOK:** 50 MINUTES

- 2 **tablespoons vegetable oil**
- 1 **pound boneless pork loin, diced**
- 1 **large sweet onion, chopped (about 2 cups)**
- 3 **cloves garlic, minced**
- 8 **cups Swanson® Chicken Broth (Regular, Natural Goodness® or Certified Organic)**
- 1 **teaspoon ground cumin**
- 1 **chipotle pepper in adobo sauce, minced**
- 1 **can (14.5 ounces) diced tomatoes, undrained**
- 1 **can (15 ounces) hominy, rinsed and drained**
- ¼ **cup chopped fresh cilantro**

1. Heat **1 tablespoon** of the oil in a 6-quart saucepot over medium-high heat. Add the pork and cook until it's well browned, stirring often. Remove the pork from the saucepot with a slotted spoon.

2. Add the remaining oil to the saucepot and reduce the heat to medium. Add the onion and garlic and cook until tender.

3. Stir in the broth, cumin, pepper, tomatoes and hominy. Heat to a boil. Return the pork to the saucepot and reduce the heat to low. Cover and cook for 35 minutes or until the pork is tender.

KITCHEN TIP

Hominy is dried white or yellow corn kernels with the germ and hull removed. When canned, it's ready to eat. Ground hominy is also known as corn grits or simply grits.

Southwest Onion Soup

MAKES: 8 SERVINGS ■ **PREP:** 10 MINUTES ■ **COOK:** 30 MINUTES

1 tablespoon olive oil

2 large Spanish onions, sliced

½ pound boneless beef chuck roast, cut into cubes

1 teaspoon ground chipotle pepper

4 cups Swanson® Beef Broth (Regular, 50% Less Sodium or Certified Organic)

1 bottle (12 fluid ounces) Mexican beer

1 can (14.5 ounces) diced tomatoes with jalapeños

1 cup frozen **or** drained, canned whole kernel corn

Tortilla chips

1 package (8 ounces) shredded Mexican cheese blend

1. Heat the oil in a 6-quart saucepot over medium-high heat. Add the onions and cook until tender.

2. Add the beef and pepper. Cook until the beef is well browned, stirring often.

3. Stir in the broth, beer, tomatoes and corn. Heat to a boil. Reduce the heat to low. Cover and cook for 15 minutes or until the beef is fork-tender.

4. Divide the soup among **8** microwavable serving bowls. Top **each** with **3** tortilla chips and **2 tablespoons** of the cheese. Microwave 2 bowls at a time on HIGH for 30 seconds or until the cheese melts. Serve immediately.

Zuppa de Farro

MAKES: 6 SERVINGS ■ **PREP:** 1 HOUR 40 MINUTES ■ **COOK:** 35 MINUTES

8 ounces whole cereal farro grain **or** quick pearl barley

4 ounces pancetta, chopped

1 small onion, sliced (about ¼ cup)

2 cloves garlic, minced

1 teaspoon dried thyme leaves, crushed

4 cups Swanson® Chicken Broth (Regular, Natural Goodness® **or** Certified Organic)

2 medium plum tomatoes, chopped (about 1 cup)

1 tablespoon chopped fresh basil leaves

¼ teaspoon ground black pepper

Parmesan cheese (optional)

1. Place the farro in a large bowl. Add water to cover and let soak for 1 hour. Drain. Place the farro in a 6-quart saucepot. Cover with 8 cups water. Heat to a boil. Cook for 30 minutes. Drain. Reserve farro.

2. In the same saucepot cook the pancetta, onion, garlic and thyme over medium heat for about 10 minutes or until well browned. Add the broth and tomatoes. Heat to a boil. Reduce the heat to low. Cook for 10 minutes. Add the farro, basil and black pepper. Cook for 10 minutes more. Serve with cheese, if desired.

KITCHEN TIP

If using quick pearl barley instead of farro, do not pre-cook. Add to the soup with the broth and tomatoes.

Pho-Style Soup

MAKES: 4 SERVINGS ■ **PREP:** 10 MINUTES ■ **COOK:** 20 MINUTES

2 tablespoons vegetable oil	3 cloves garlic, minced
1 pound boneless beef round steak, cut into thin strips	¼ teaspoon ground cloves
4 cups Swanson® Beef Broth (Regular, 50% Less Sodium or Certified Organic)	¼ teaspoon ground black pepper
	Hot cooked soba noodles
1 tablespoon finely minced fresh ginger	1 tablespoon finely chopped green onion

1. Heat the oil in a 12-inch skillet. Add the beef and stir-fry until it's well browned, stirring often. Remove the beef from the skillet with a slotted spoon.

2. Heat the broth, ginger, garlic, cloves and black pepper in a 4-quart saucepan over high heat to a boil. Reduce the heat to low. Cover and cook for 10 minutes. Return the beef to the saucepan. Cook for 5 minutes.

3. Serve the soup mixture over noodles and garnish with green onion.

KITCHEN TIP

The beef will be easier to slice into thin strips if you freeze it for at least one hour.

Spanish Chicken and Rice Soup

MAKES: 6 SERVINGS ■ **PREP:** 15 MINUTES ■ **COOK:** 50 MINUTES

2 tablespoons vegetable oil	8 cups Swanson® Chicken Broth (Regular, Natural Goodness® or Certified Organic)
1 pound skinless, boneless chicken thighs, cut into cubes	1 can (14.5 ounces) diced tomatoes, undrained
1 large sweet onion, chopped (about 2 cups)	1 package (5 ounces) saffron yellow rice mix with seasoning
2 cloves garlic, minced	½ cup pitted green olives, sliced
¼ teaspoon crushed red pepper	¼ cup sliced fresh basil leaves

1. Heat **1 tablespoon** of the oil in a 6-quart saucepot over medium-high heat. Add the chicken and cook until it's well browned, stirring often. Remove the chicken from the saucepot with a slotted spoon.

2. Add the remaining oil to the saucepot and reduce the heat to medium. Add the onion, garlic and red pepper and cook for 3 minutes.

3. Stir in the broth and tomatoes. Heat to a boil. Reduce the heat to low. Cover and cook for 15 minutes.

4. Stir in the rice and olives. Return the chicken to the saucepot. Cover and cook for 20 minutes or until the chicken is cooked through and the rice is done. Stir in the basil.

Mexican Chicken-in-a-Pot Soup

MAKES: 6 SERVINGS ■ **PREP:** 10 MINUTES ■ **COOK:** 30 MINUTES

- 1 rotisserie cooked chicken (about 1½ pounds)
- 2 tablespoons vegetable oil
- 2 medium onions, chopped (about 2 cups)
- 2 large green peppers, chopped (about 2 cups)
- 2 cloves garlic, minced
- 2 teaspoons ground cumin
- 2 teaspoons dried oregano leaves, crushed
- 7 cups Swanson® Chicken Broth (Regular, Natural Goodness® **or** Certified Organic)
- 1 can (14.5 ounces) diced tomatoes, undrained
- 1 tablespoon lime juice

  Hot cooked rice

1. Remove the skin and bones from the chicken. Shred about **half** of the chicken meat using 2 forks or pull apart with your fingers to yield about 2 cups.

2. Heat the oil in a 4-quart saucepan over medium heat. Add the onions, peppers, garlic, cumin and oregano. Cook for 5 minutes or until the vegetables are tender-crisp.

3. Stir in the broth and tomatoes. Heat to a boil. Reduce the heat to low. Cook for 10 minutes. Add the chicken and cook for 10 minutes or until the vegetables are tender.

4. Stir in the lime juice. Spoon rice into **each** of **6** serving bowls. Ladle the soup around **each** serving of rice.

Thai Roasted Squash Soup

MAKES: 6 SERVINGS ■ **PREP:** 35 MINUTES ■ **COOK:** 50 MINUTES

2 tablespoons vegetable oil

2 teaspoons curry powder

1 butternut squash (about 2½ pounds), peeled, seeded and cut into 2-inch pieces (about 6 cups)

1 large sweet onion, cut into eighths

1 tablespoon chopped fresh ginger

3 cups Swanson® Chicken Broth (Regular, Natural Goodness® **or** Certified Organic)

1 can (15 ounces) cream of coconut

3 tablespoons chopped fresh cilantro

1. Heat the oven to 425°F.

2. Stir the oil and curry in a large bowl. Add the squash and onion and toss to coat. Spread the vegetables onto a shallow-sided baking pan.

3. Bake for 25 minutes or until the vegetables are golden brown, stirring occasionally.

4. Put the vegetables and ginger in a 3-quart saucepan. Stir in the broth and cream of coconut. Heat to a boil. Reduce the heat to low. Cook for 20 minutes or until the vegetables are tender.

5. Spoon ⅓ of the soup mixture into an electric blender or food processor container. Cover and blend until smooth. Pour into a large bowl. Repeat the blending process twice more with the remaining soup mixture. Return all of the puréed mixture to the saucepan. Cook over medium heat until the mixture is hot. Season to taste. Divide the soup among **6** serving bowls. Sprinkle each serving of soup with cilantro.

Roasted Cauliflower Soup with Curry and Ginger

MAKES: 8 SERVINGS ■ **PREP:** 10 MINUTES ■ **BAKE:** 30 MINUTES ■ **COOK:** 25 MINUTES

- 1 head cauliflower (about 1 pound), trimmed and separated into flowerets
- 2 large parsnips, thickly sliced
- 2 tablespoons olive oil
- 1 large sweet onion, sliced (about 2 cups)
- 6 cups Swanson® Chicken Broth (Regular, Natural Goodness® or Certified Organic)
- ⅓ bunch fresh cilantro (about ½ ounce)
- 1 tablespoon minced fresh ginger
- ½ teaspoon curry powder
- ½ teaspoon ground cumin
- ½ cup plain yogurt

  Optional garnishes: cooked crumbled bacon, black trumpet mushrooms, cilantro oil, flat leaf parsley

1. Heat the oven to 425°F. Place the cauliflower and the parsnips in a 17×11-inch roasting pan. Pour **1 tablespoon** of the oil over the vegetables. Toss to coat. Bake for 30 minutes or until the vegetables are tender.

2. Heat the remaining oil in an 8-quart saucepot. Add the onion and cook until tender. Add the broth, cilantro, ginger, curry, cumin and cauliflower mixture. Heat to a boil. Reduce the heat to low. Cover and cook for 15 minutes or until hot. Stir in the yogurt.

3. Place ⅓ of the broth mixture in an electric blender or food processor container. Cover and blend until smooth. Pour the mixture into a large bowl. Repeat the blending process twice more with the remaining broth mixture. Return all of the puréed mixture to the saucepot. Cook over medium heat for 5 minutes or until hot. Season to taste. Pour the soup through a sieve, if desired.

Spicy Verde Chicken & Bean Chili

MAKES: 6 SERVINGS ■ **PREP:** 10 MINUTES ■ **COOK:** 40 MINUTES

- 2 tablespoons butter
- 1 large onion, chopped (about 1 cup)
- ¼ teaspoon garlic powder **or** 2 cloves garlic, minced
- 1 tablespoon all-purpose flour
- 2 cups Swanson® Chicken Broth (Regular, Natural Goodness® **or** Certified Organic)
- 2 cups shredded cooked chicken

- 1 can (about 15 ounces) small white beans, undrained
- 1 can (4 ounces) chopped green chiles, drained
- 1 teaspoon ground cumin
- 1 teaspoon jalapeño hot pepper sauce
- 6 flour tortillas (8-inch), warmed

  Shredded Monterey Jack cheese (optional)

  Chopped fresh cilantro (optional)

1. Heat the butter in a 12-inch skillet over medium heat. Add the onion and garlic powder. Cook and stir until the onion is tender.

2. Stir the flour into the skillet. Cook and stir for 2 minutes. Gradually stir in the broth. Cook and stir until the mixture boils and thickens.

3. Stir in the chicken, beans, chiles, cumin and hot sauce. Heat to a boil. Reduce the heat to low. Cook for 20 minutes, stirring occasionally.

4. Line **each** of **6** serving bowls with the tortillas. Divide the chili among the bowls. Serve **each** topped with cheese and cilantro, if desired.

Chipotle Black Bean Soup with Avocado Cream

MAKES: 8 SERVINGS ■ **PREP:** 10 MINUTES ■ **COOK:** 40 MINUTES

2 tablespoons olive oil

4 large carrots, diced (about 2 cups)

1 large sweet onion, chopped (about 2 cups)

1 canned chipotle pepper in adobo sauce, minced

4 cups Swanson® Chicken Broth (Regular, Natural Goodness® or Certified Organic)

3 cans (about 15 ounces each) black beans, rinsed and drained

1 small ripe avocado, pitted, peeled and cut into cubes (about ½ cup)

¼ cup sour cream

2 tablespoons chopped fresh cilantro leaves

1 tablespoon lemon juice

1. Heat the oil in a 4-quart saucepan. Add the carrots and onion and cook until tender-crisp. Add the pepper and cook for 1 minute.

2. Stir the broth and beans into the saucepan. Heat to a boil. Reduce the heat to low. Cook for 25 minutes.

3. Mash the avocado with a fork in a small bowl until smooth. Stir in the sour cream, cilantro and lemon juice and set it aside.

4. Purée the soup mixture in batches until smooth. Return all of the puréed mixture to the saucepot. Cook over medium heat until the mixture is hot. Season to taste. Divide the soup among **8** serving bowls. Top **each** serving of soup with some of the avocado cream.

Yellow Split Pea Soup with Andouille Sausage

MAKES: 6 SERVINGS ■ **PREP:** 15 MINUTES ■ **COOK:** 4 HOURS

5 cups Swanson® Chicken Broth (Regular, Natural Goodness® or Certified Organic)

3 medium carrots, thinly sliced (2 cups)

3 stalks celery, thinly sliced (1½ cups)

1 medium red onion, finely chopped (about 1 cup)

¼ cup chopped fresh parsley

4 cloves garlic, chopped

1 bay leaf

2 cups dried yellow split peas

6 ounces andouille sausage, casing removed and sliced **or** 1 package (16 ounces) smoked andouille sausage, diced (about 1½ cups)

1. Place the broth, carrots, celery, red onion, parsley, garlic, bay leaf, peas and sausage in a 3½- to 6-quart slow cooker. Cover and cook on HIGH for 4 hours* or until done. Remove the bay leaf.

2. Place ⅓ of the broth mixture into an electric blender or food processor container. Cover and blend until almost smooth. Pour the mixture into a large bowl. Repeat the blending process twice more with the remaining broth mixture. Return all of the puréed mixture to a 3-quart saucepan. Cook over medium heat until the mixture is hot.

*Or on LOW for 8 hours

Fennel Soup au Gratin

MAKES: 8 SERVINGS ■ **PREP:** 15 MINUTES ■ **COOK:** 6 HOURS

8 cups Swanson® Beef Broth
   (Regular, 50% Less Sodium
   or Certified Organic)

2 tablespoons dry sherry

2 teaspoons dried thyme leaves,
   crushed

3 tablespoons butter

1 bulb fennel, sliced (about
   4 cups)

2 medium onions, sliced (about
   4 cups)

8 ounces French bread, sliced
   ½-inch thick

½ cup shredded Italian blend
   cheese

1. Stir the broth, sherry, thyme, butter, fennel and onions in a 5½-quart slow cooker. Cover and cook on HIGH for 6 hours.

2. Just before serving, top **each** bread slice with **1 tablespoon** of the cheese. Place the bread on a baking sheet. Broil 4 inches from the heat for 1 minute or until golden.

3. Divide the soup mixture among **8** serving bowls. Top **each** serving of soup with a cheese toast.

Chicken & Herb Dumplings

MAKES: 8 SERVINGS ■ **PREP:** 20 MINUTES ■ **COOK:** 7 TO 8 HOURS 45 MINUTES

2 **pounds skinless, boneless chicken (breasts and/ or thighs), cut into 1-inch pieces**

5 **medium carrots, cut diagonally into 1-inch pieces (about 2½ cups)**

4 **stalks celery, cut diagonally into 1-inch pieces (about 2 cups)**

2 **cups frozen whole kernel corn**

3½ **cups Swanson® Chicken Broth (Regular, Natural Goodness® or Certified Organic)**

¼ **teaspoon ground black pepper**

½ **cup water**

¼ **cup all-purpose flour**

2 **cups all-purpose baking mix**

⅔ **cup milk**

1 **tablespoon chopped fresh rosemary or 1 teaspoon dried rosemary leaves, crushed**

1. Place the chicken, carrots, celery and corn in a 6-quart slow cooker. Stir in the broth and black pepper. Cover and cook on LOW for 7 to 8 hours* or until chicken is cooked through.

2. Stir the water into the flour in a small bowl until smooth and stir the mixture into the cooker. Turn the heat to HIGH. Cover and cook for 5 minutes or until the mixture boils and thickens.

3. Meanwhile, stir together the baking mix, milk and rosemary with a fork in a small bowl until the ingredients are mixed. Drop the batter by rounded tablespoonsful over the chicken mixture. Tilt the cooker lid to vent and cook for 40 minutes or until dumplings are cooked in the center.

*Or on HIGH for 4 to 5 hours

White Bean with Fennel Soup

MAKES: 6 SERVINGS ■ **PREP:** 15 MINUTES ■ **COOK:** 7 TO 8 HOURS

4 cups Swanson® Vegetable Broth (Regular **or** Certified Organic)

1/8 teaspoon ground black pepper

1 small bulb fennel (about 1/2 pound), trimmed and sliced (about 2 cups)

1 small onion, chopped (about 1/2 cup)

2 cloves garlic, minced

1 package (10 ounces) frozen leaf spinach

1 can (14.5 ounces) diced tomatoes, undrained

1 can (about 16 ounces) white kidney (cannellini) beans, undrained

1. Stir the broth, black pepper, fennel, onion and garlic in a 5½- to 6-quart slow cooker.

2. Cover and cook on LOW for 6 to 7 hours.

3. Add the spinach, tomatoes and beans. Turn the heat to HIGH. Cover and cook for 1 hour more or until the vegetables are tender.

Southwestern Chicken & White Bean Soup

MAKES: 6 SERVINGS ■ **PREP:** 15 MINUTES ■ **COOK:** 8 TO 10 HOURS 5 MINUTES

- 1 tablespoon vegetable oil
- 1 pound skinless, boneless chicken breasts, cut into 1-inch pieces
- 1¾ cups Swanson® Chicken Broth (Regular, Natural Goodness® **or** Certified Organic)
- 1 cup Pace® Chunky Salsa
- 3 cloves garlic, minced
- 2 teaspoons ground cumin
- 1 can (about 16 ounces) small white beans, rinsed and drained
- 1 cup frozen whole kernel corn
- 1 small onion, chopped (about ½ cup)

1. Heat the oil in a 10-inch skillet over medium-high heat. Add the chicken and cook until it's well browned, stirring often.

2. Stir the broth, salsa, garlic, cumin, beans, corn and onion in a 3½-quart slow cooker. Add the chicken.

3. Cover and cook on LOW for 8 to 10 hours* or until the chicken is cooked through.

*Or on HIGH for 4 to 5 hours

Slow-Simmered Chicken Rice Soup

MAKES: 8 SERVINGS ■ **PREP:** 10 MINUTES ■ **COOK:** 7 TO 8 HOURS 15 MINUTES

½ cup **uncooked** wild rice

½ cup **uncooked** regular long-grain white rice

1 tablespoon vegetable oil

5¼ cups Swanson® Chicken Broth (Regular, Natural Goodness® **or** Certified Organic)

2 teaspoons dried thyme leaves, crushed

¼ teaspoon crushed red pepper

2 stalks celery, coarsely chopped (about 1 cup)

1 medium onion, chopped (about ½ cup)

1 pound skinless, boneless chicken breasts, cut into cubes

Sour cream (optional)

Chopped green onions (optional)

1. Stir the wild rice, white rice and oil in a 3½-quart slow cooker. Cover and cook on HIGH for 15 minutes.

2. Stir the broth, thyme, red pepper, celery, onion and chicken into the cooker. Turn the heat to LOW. Cover and cook on LOW for 7 to 8 hours* or until the chicken is cooked through.

3. Serve with the sour cream and green onions, if desired.

*Or on HIGH for 4 to 5 hours

TIME-SAVING TIP

*Speed preparation by substituting 3 cans (4.5 ounces **each**) Swanson® Premium Chunk Chicken Breast, drained, for the raw chicken.*

Barley and Lentil Soup

MAKES: 8 SERVINGS ■ **PREP:** 10 MINUTES ■ **COOK:** 8 TO 9 HOURS

8 cups Swanson® Beef Broth
  (Regular, 50% Less Sodium
  or Certified Organic)
2 cloves garlic, minced
1 teaspoon dried oregano
  leaves, crushed

4 large carrots, sliced
  (about 3 cups)
1 medium onion, chopped
  (about 1 cup)
½ cup dried lentils
½ cup **uncooked** pearl barley

1. Stir the broth, garlic, oregano, carrots, onion, lentils and barley in a
3½- to 6-quart slow cooker.

2. Cover and cook on LOW for 8 to 9 hours* or until the lentils and barley
are tender.

Or on HIGH for 4 to 5 hours